SAINT MAXIMILIAN KOLBE

St. Maximilian Kolbe
Friar Minor Conventual
1894-1941

SAINT MAXIMILIAN KOLBE

KNIGHT OF THE IMMACULATA

By

Fr. Jeremiah J. Smith, O.F.M. CONV.

"Greater love than this no man hath, that a man lay down his life for his friends." —John 13:15

TAN BOOKS AND PUBLISHERS, INC.
Rockford, Illinois 61105

Nihil Obstat: Vincent M. Mayer, O.F.M. Conv.
                Censor Librorum
                Syracuse, New York
                April 20, 1951

Imprimi Potest: Francis Edic, O.F.M. Conv.
                Minister Provincial
                Syracuse, New York
                April 22, 1951

Imprimatur: ✟ Walter Foery
                Bishop of Syracuse
                April 24, 1951

Originally published in 1952 by Conventual Franciscan Publications, St. Anthony-on-Hudson, Rensselaer, New York. Retypeset and republished in 1998 by TAN Books and Publishers, Inc.

Cover illustration used courtesy of Franciscan Marytown Press, Libertyville, Illinois. Grateful acknowledgment to Franciscan Marytown for use of several of the pictures in the text, and to Ave Maria Institute, publisher of *I Knew Blessed Maximilian Kolbe*, by J. Mlodozeniec, for picture on page 105.

ISBN 0-89555-619-7

Library of Congress Catalog Card No.: 98-60480

Printed and bound in the United States of America.

TAN BOOKS AND PUBLISHERS, INC.
P.O. Box 424
Rockford, Illinois 61105
1998

"Modern times are dominated by Satan and will be more so in the future. The conflict with Hell cannot be engaged by men, even the most clever. The Immaculata alone has from God the promise of victory over Satan."

—St. Maximilian Kolbe

The author of this book declares in everything herein contained his filial submission to the decrees of Pope Urban VIII and to the norms of the Holy Roman Catholic Church, of which he is a devoted subject. He does not allege or exact any other faith than human, based upon the authority of the individual witness summoned.

CONTENTS

St. Maximilian Maria Kolbe founded the Knights of the Immaculata to conquer all souls for Christ through Mary Immaculate. This photo shows him as a young priest in 1919.

INTRODUCTION

ANOTHER name can be inscribed on the list of great Apostles of Our Lady. Side by side with such illustrious devotees of the Blessed Mother as St. Bernard, Duns Scotus, St. Louis Grignion De Montfort and Ven. William Chaminade stands also St. Maximilian Kolbe, a Friar Minor Conventual. His distinct contribution to the spread of Mary's glory is characterized in a title which he gave to one of his publications: *The Knight of the Immaculata*. In this title is marvelously epitomized his life's work, as well as his ideal.

In his actual accomplishments, he spread the glory of Mary Immaculate with a chivalry worthy of the most ardent of medieval knights. He had one "fixed idea": to show all men in all places how to love the Immaculata without limit. To realize this ideal, no sacrifice was too difficult: hard work, sleepless nights, misunderstanding, persecution, and even death itself.

In one of his writings, St. Maximilian has left us a biographical note in which he says: "I was still a young boy when I promised myself to take the field for the Blessed Virgin, without knowing then how I would do this or what arms I would use." This took place when he was thirteen or fourteen years old. When he died in 1941 on the vigil of the Assumption in a concentration camp at Oswiecim—Auschwitz—he could look back over his life with satisfaction and realize that he had fulfilled this promise as faithfully as possible. His death itself was martyrdom, not in the usual sense of the word, but a martyrdom of charity. Following the example of Christ, he gave his life for his neighbor: "Greater love than this no man hath, that a man lay down his life for his friends." (*John* 15:13).

In his lifetime of forty-seven years, St. Maximilian Kolbe founded two cities which he dedicated to the Lady of his love, the Immaculata. Following his contagious example, hundreds of young men dedicated their lives to Mary's Divine Son in poverty, chastity and obedience. He spread the glory of the Immaculata not only among souls consecrated to God, but also in the hearts of millions of the laity by establishing his Militia of Mary Immaculate. He wrote about her in his numerous newspapers and reviews. He preached about her in Europe and Asia. Above all, he ardently gave only what he himself felt. He was the Knight of the Immaculata.

Here is his story, the story of a meek and

insignificant figure amid the giants of our generation, the story of a chronic victim of tuberculosis, the story of a pair of empty hands holding limitless ambitions, of a short lifetime marked by incredible deeds and climaxed with an heroic death in the foulest of all Nazi concentration camps.

SAINT
MAXIMILIAN
KOLBE

Chapter 1

THE KOLBE FAMILY

JANUARY 8, 1894, was the birthday of Raymond Kolbe, the future Franciscan who would be known to the world as St. Maximilian Kolbe. There were four other boys in the Kolbe family, two of whom died at an early age. The other two were Francis, older than Raymond, and Joseph, the youngest in the family, who as Father Alphonse became the constant companion and co-worker of Father Maximilian.

At the time of Raymond's birth, the family was living at Zdunska Wola, a small village near Lodz, Poland. Shortly after this Julius Kolbe, the father, a weaver by trade, moved with his family to Pabianice in search of better living conditions. However, the weaving business prospered no better there, so the Kolbes opened a delicatessen store, which for the most part was run by Mrs. Kolbe and her boys.

Both Mr. and Mrs. Kolbe were solidly religious people. In fact, Mrs. Kolbe, born Maria Dombrowska, as a young girl several years before her marriage had intended to become a nun. As it was, after their sons were well on their own, both mother and father made a pilgrimage to the famous Polish shrine at Czestochowa and there by mutual agreement made a vow of chastity at the foot of the Immaculata's statue. It was, however, only after the First World War that Mrs. Kolbe could see her way clear to become part of a religious congregation of sisters. Until her death in March, 1946, she could still be seen begging for her community along the streets and in the offices and workshops of Krakow. Mr. Kolbe went to live with the Franciscan Order of Friars Minor Conventual, probably becoming a secular oblate. But he left for the First World War, and it seems that he was mistakenly executed as a traitor in 1917 or 1918.

Chapter 2

THE TWO CROWNS

RAYMOND'S boyhood days were not much different from those of any normal Polish youth. He was a lively boy, quick-witted and just a trifle headstrong. But his mother at one time pointed out that, of all her sons, Raymond was the most obedient, humble and submissive to her and his father. When Mr. Kolbe went off to work, she said, it was Raymond who became her little handyman, helping with the cooking, the cleaning and the many chores of the house. This son of hers, she related, distinguished himself from his two brothers even in the way he accepted punishment for some minor offense. Of his own accord he would bring the whip and bend over the chair unhesitatingly; then, after he had been chastised, he would thank his parents and would return the whip to its place.

Evidently the lad often tried the patience of his mother with his boyish pranks. On one occasion, he so grated on her nerves that she shouted in a fit of excitement: "I do not know what will become of you!"

After this incident there was a noticeable change in Raymond's whole behavior. He seemed very different and even mysterious at times. Mother Kolbe began to wonder at this sudden transformation. She also noticed that very frequently thereafter he would slip off to the room in which the Kolbes had set up an altar of Our Lady, and there he would pray for long periods. Often she observed that when he returned from that room his eyes were red from tears.

His mother was intrigued by this. She restrained her inquisitiveness for some time, until finally she had to put the question to him squarely: "See here, Raymond, what is wrong with you? Why do you cry like a little girl?" The boy lowered his head and definitely indicated that he did not wish to answer this question. Mrs. Kolbe was not the mother to be put off so easily. She pressed the issue:

"My child," wisely she went on, "you must tell your mother everything; do not be disobedient."

The boy earnestly avowed that he did not intend to be disobedient. In tears and almost trembling, he went on to tell his mother: "Mama, when you said to me: 'Raymond, I do not know what will become of you,' it upset me very much, and so I went to ask the Blessed Virgin just

Above: Mrs. Kolbe— a simple, devout woman who taught her sons to love Mary Immaculate even more than they loved her. This photo was taken in 1941. *Left:* Young Raymond Kolbe in 1907.

what I would become. Later, at church, I asked her once again. Then she appeared to me, holding two crowns, a white one and a red one. Tenderly she looked at me and asked me which one I would choose; the white signified that I would always be pure, and the red that I would die a martyr. Then I answered the Blessed Virgin: 'I choose both!' She smiled and disappeared."

Both mother and son looked at each other. There was a moment of silence. Then the boy went on to explain naively that thereafter when he went to church with her and his father, it seemed to him that he did not go with them, but rather with the Blessed Virgin and St. Joseph!

Indeed his mother was impressed. Nor did she hesitate to believe the boy. In later years, when she told this story, she added that the radical change in him was proof enough that her son was telling the truth.

"From that day on," she said, "he was no longer the same. Often, with beaming face, he would speak to me of martyrdom. This was his great dream."

Chapter 3

MINOR SEMINARY AND NOVITIATE

AT the time of this episode, Raymond was just ten years old. About three years later a mission was given at Pabianice by the Franciscan Conventual Fathers. At the close of the mission one of the priests announced that his superiors had opened a minor seminary at Lwow for youths desiring to consecrate themselves to Our Lord in the Order of St. Francis.

Raymond and his elder brother Francis were delighted to hear this news, for both of them had been harboring the idea of becoming priests. Without delay, they set the proposition before their mother and father. We are not aware of the details of this incident, but we do know that their parents put no obstacles in the way of their two older sons' becoming priests. Both boys had enough education to permit their entrance into the seminary. Francis, as the older of the two, had been given the opportunity to attend the local commercial school. Raymond was not so fortunate. He was needed at home. But with the help of the local parish priest and the neighborhood druggist, he was prepared sufficiently well to pass the second class examination at the commercial school at the same time as his brother.

Since the latter part of the eighteenth century, Poland had been divided among the countries of Prussia, Austria and Russia. Now Pabianice was located in the Russian zone; whereas the seminary was in Austrian territory. Since free passage through the zones was frowned upon and even forbidden, it was necessary for the boys to make their way secretly across the frontier. This was the first time in their lives they had ever traveled alone, but their youthful spirit of adventure and the thrill of entering a seminary goaded them on to overcome all obstacles. Fortunately, their journey was unimpeded. In short order, they found themselves at Lwow, where they were to remain for the next few years and where they were given their basic training for the priesthood.

Time passed quickly. Raymond especially, with a passion for mathematics and science, gave definite signs to his teachers that he was capable of advancing to the higher studies of philosophy and theology. But if he grew in the knowledge of the intellectual sciences, he also advanced in the wisdom of the spiritual life. His vision and love of Our Lady never left him. It was during this era that he promised to be a Knight of Our Lady—to win souls for her as a soldier on a field of battle. However, it was precisely this "fixed idea" of his that brought about the second crisis of his life.

At the time of this crisis Raymond was about sixteen. It was the day before he was to enter the novitiate and to be invested with the black habit of the Franciscan Conventual Order. The poor boy suffered a diabolic temptation, which was all the more dangerous in that it was clothed with reasons and persuasive arguments derived from a seemingly holy intention. What was this temptation?

We have seen that Raymond had consecrated his life to Our Lady; he had promised to be a soldier of Our Lady. But how? There was the temptation. He was persuaded that he could better fulfill his dedication to the Blessed Virgin by a military career than in the religious life. As a matter of fact, he even suggested this idea to Francis. Until this time his brother had been well disposed to begin his year of trial. But Raymond's arguments were persuasive. The two boys were on the point of going to the Provincial to tell him that they did not wish to enter the Order. But Providence intervened. The doorbell of the seminary rang. In a few minutes, the

Provincial called them to tell them that their mother was in the reception room waiting to visit with them. This was unexpected. She immediately explained that she had come to give them very heartening news: their younger brother, Joseph, had decided to become a religious, and as a result of this, both she and Mr. Kolbe could now also dedicate their lives to God in a religious order! What else went on in that room that day we do not know. But of this much we are certain: as soon as Mrs. Kolbe left the visiting room, both boys went to the Provincial to tell him that they wished to enter the novitiate. The following day Raymond became Friar Maximilian Kolbe.

Chapter 4

STUDIES IN ROME

ON September 11, 1911, Friar Maximilian pronounced his vows of poverty, chastity and obedience for three years in the Order of Friars Minor Conventual. A year later, his superiors, recognizing his exceptional talent, decided to send him to the Gregorian University in Rome.

Ordinarily, this honor would have delighted a seminary student. But not Friar Maximilian! It seems that already at this early date his health was not too good. Whether he had begun to show signs of the tuberculosis which he certainly had later we cannot say. At any rate he asked his Provincial to strike his name from the list of students selected for Rome, offering as a reason the possibility that his health could not stand the Italian climate. This was his own decision; that much he knew. That same night, as he lay in bed, he realized in mental agony that in this decision he was placing his own will before God's, which had been made known to him by the desire of his Superior. "Surely," he thought to himself, "it is better to throw myself into the hands of God and to obey blindly." The following morning he went to the Provincial and placed the entire affair solely in his hands, stating humbly and sincerely that he was prepared to accept whatever his Superior wished. The Provincial decided that he should go to Rome, and Friar Maximilian obeyed unquestioningly! In later years, recalling this incident, Maximilian asked this question: "In truth, what would have happened if Father Provincial had decided according to my reasons? Would there have been a *Knight of the Immaculata* today? Would there have been such a place as the City of the Immaculata? Would we have had the good fortune of working to make known the glories of the Immaculata? Is not then the glory of obedience blind submission to the Lord?" All through his life he would show this same conscientious regard for holy obedience. It became his characteristic virtue.

Rome, too, proved to be not only a school for intellectual progress but also for his spiritual development. He had the good fortune to spend his years in Rome under the rectorship and direction of one of the most illustrious religious in the Holy City, Father Stephen Ignudi, O.F.M. Conv. As a seminarian, Friar Maximilian imbibed fully the spirituality of this truly ascetic priest. This was one of the contacts which made a life-long impression upon him. By the first of November, 1914, the young religious pronounced his solemn vows; on this occasion there was no hesitation. A year later, October 22, at the age of twenty-one, he received his doctorate in philosophy at the Gregorian University, where it is recalled that he contributed much to scientific projects. In the course of the following years at Rome, he was ordained sub-deacon in 1916, priest in 1918, and on April 29, 1918, he said his first Mass. A year later, July, 1919, Father Maximilian received his doctor's degree in theology at the International Seraphic College of his Order.

This in brief is the history of Father Maximilian's stay in Rome. His life there, considered externally, was the life of any devout young man studying for the priesthood. Interiorly, however, his life is the revelation of an extraordinary soul. During these years he developed fully the determination to do the will of God in all his actions and to bring all souls to Christ through the Immaculata. Nor did he intend that his relation to Christ and His Blessed Mother would be one of words only. Above all he was a man of action. His whole life would be proof of this. Later on, in his writings, he revealed how at this time he made an agreement with St. Therese the Little Flower, who was not yet canonized: "I shall pray that you may be raised to the glory of the altars, but on the condition that you will take charge of all my future conquests." And how many were those conquests to be!

He was not for a moment hesitant or affrighted where it was a question of bringing glory to God. No obstacle was discouraging enough to deter him. One of his closest friends in Rome, Father Pal, related that Father Maximilian would on occasion rush headlong into discussion with the anti-Christian street orators in the public squares. In the course of one of these discussions, a pseudo-intellectual became angered at the way this boyish-looking religious was driving him against the wall. He thought he would frighten Maximilian by shouting, "Son, I am a doctor of philosophy!" He was immediately answered, "I am also." The gentleman looked at the young religious in amazement and quickly began to change his tune. Then, patiently, Maximilian answered the man's arguments and left him there abashed and astonished.

Chapter 5

THE MILITIA OF
MARY IMMACULATE

BUT if we are really to appreciate this man of spiritual action, we must see him at work, organizing and founding The Militia of Mary Immaculate. In fact, this was to be the vehicle of all his future conquests for Our Lady.

The need for an organization dedicated to the Immaculata was the result of several incidents which occurred in Rome in 1917. This year saw the second centenary celebration of Freemasonry, and true to form they chose the Holy City of Rome as the theatre of sacrilegious demonstrations. In front of the Vatican, the Freemasons paraded signs which read "Satan must reign in the Vatican. The Pope will be his slave." Scurrilous pamphlets directed against the Holy Father were distributed among the people.

Friar Maximilian, who was not yet a priest, saw all this and immediately hit upon the idea of forming an association which would combat not only these Freemasons, but also all protagonists of the devil. He knew that Our Lady is the key to the conquest of Satan. Maximilian would write: "Modern times are dominated by Satan and will be more so in the future. The conflict with Hell cannot be engaged by men, even the most clever. The Immaculata alone has from God the promise of victory over Satan."

Now our young Franciscan was not the religious who would act hastily and with undue consideration. In order to reassure himself that his idea was really in agreement with the will of Our Lady, he went and placed the whole matter before his spiritual director, who agreed perfectly to the wholesomeness of the plan.

Another factor cemented his determination to begin The Militia of Mary Immaculate. It was a discourse which was given to the students of the seminary by Father Stephen Ignudi. The Rector of the Franciscan Seminary narrated the story of Our Lady's appearance to the celebrated Hebrew, Alphonse Ratisbonne, and his subsequent conversion, all of which was brought about through the Miraculous Medal, which Ratisbonne kept on his person. When Friar Maximilian heard this, he thought to himself that, if Mary would soften the heart of this non-Christian through her Miraculous Medal, why would she not do the same for all obstinate hearts.

During the summer of 1917, Friar Maximil-

ian for the first time disclosed his idea of founding an association of Our Lady's servants. His
friends, Friar Jerome Biasi and Father Joseph Pal,
recently ordained to the priesthood, were his
audience. In opening his heart, he reminded
them that they might discuss their co-operation
with their spiritual directors, so that all would
then be sure that it was the will of God. A few
other friends were soon invited to join in establishing The Militia of Mary Immaculate.

Finally, with the permission of the rector of
the seminary, seven friars held their first meet-
ing to begin formally the Militia. It was on
October 17, just four days after the appearance
of Our Lady to the children at Fatima. The cer-
emony was simple. Six Franciscan seminarians,
among whom was Friar Maximilian, and one
priest, met in one of the cells of the seminary.
They stood before a statue of the Blessed Virgin with its two lighted candles. Friar Maximilian read from a small sheet of paper the
program for the Militia. Then he asked all of
his confreres to sign it. This finished, they went
to the chapel where the priest of the group
blessed the Miraculous Medal and placed it on
the first members of the Militia.

Although simple in verbal expression, the program outlined for the new association by the
seven Franciscans was magnificent in spiritual

purport. It was a vast undertaking: *to conquer for Christ all souls in the entire world to the end of time—through the Immaculate Mother.*

How did they hope that this was to be done? Theirs was a simple and sane plan. Each member was to dedicate himself voluntarily and completely to Mary Immaculate in order to belong to her entirely as her property and possession. Next, as a result of their personal sanctification and the sanctification of others, they were to labor, each according to the grace given him, for the conversion of sinners, heretics, schismatics, infidels, Communists—in fact, for the conversion of all enemies of the Church. Each member was to strive to induce others to join the Militia. These new recruits could be enrolled simply by having their name inscribed in the register of a canonically erected Union. Then, after they had made their act of consecration to Our Lady according to the set form, they were to wear the Miraculous Medal and recite at least once a day the following prayer:

> "O Mary, conceived without sin, pray for us who have recourse to thee and for those who do not have recourse to thee, especially for the enemies of the Church, and for those recommended to thee."

Friar Maximilian had a universal ideal in view. He did not visualize the Militia as limited to Franciscans, or to Poles, or to Italians, but rather it was his intention that it should embrace *all* nations. He hoped that the Knights of Mary would be permeated with a "fixed idea": to live, work, suffer, and, if need be, to die for Mary Immaculate.

The first period of activity of the Militia of Mary Immaculate consisted in prayer and the distribution of the Miraculous Medal. Before 1917 ended there were already as many as twenty-five members; by 1920 these had increased to 450; by 1926 there were 84,225, and by 1939, 691,219. Their number grew to be more than two million.

Intent upon obedience to the Church, Friar Maximilian did nothing without the permission of his superiors. The Militia of Mary Immaculate obtained the approval and blessing of Pope Benedict XV on April 4, 1918. His Eminence Cardinal Pompilj, on January 2, 1922, canonically established the Militia as a Pious Union. Four years later, Pope Pius XI conferred upon it many indulgences, saying: "The Militia of Mary Immaculate has already produced such an abundance of spiritual works that it justly merits a pledge of our Pontifical benevolence." On April 23, 1927, the same Pope elevated the Militia to the status of a Primary Union with the privilege of aggregating to itself affiliated unions erected elsewhere in the world. As a result, Father Maximilian's dream of world conquest for Mary made great progress toward realization; units of the Militia were formed in Italy, Poland, Romania, Holland, Belgium, America and Japan.

Chapter 6

TRUST IN GOD AND OUR LADY

THE growth and ultimate success of The Militia of Mary Immaculate was due primarily to the energy and sanctity of Friar Maximilian. Its beginnings were faced with almost insurmountable obstacles. A little over a year after the memorable day of October 17, two of his six companions died. As for the others, they did not seem to have the same vibrant enthusiasm which fired the soul of Father Maximilian.

When he left Rome as a priest in the summer of 1919 to return to Poland, it was as if he had to begin alone and all over again to disseminate his ideal. He arrived in Poland in August, 1919. By October he was appointed Professor of Theology at the Franciscan Seminary in Krakow. He began to teach, but did not remain at it long. By November he was in a hospital in Krakow; he was suffering from frequent hemorrhages, showing definite signs of tuberculosis.

Father Maximilian's health had never been too

good. The fact that he could accomplish so much in the following years despite poor health is a miracle of sorts in itself. Even while yet a student at Rome he suffered from the initial stages of tuberculosis, so much so that his superiors had to send him away for extended vacations. But his strong trust in Divine Providence overcame this physical weakness.

Faith in God carried him through to accomplish wonders. Typical of his faith and trust in God and Our Lady in the face of illness is the following incident which had taken place while he was just a young student in Rome in 1914: At that time he had an abscess on the thumb of his right hand. The doctor decided that it was necessary to amputate it because the bone had already begun to decay. The day before the operation, the Rector of the seminary gave Friar Maximilian some blessed water from Lourdes, which he immediately applied to the infected finger. When the young cleric arrived at the hospital the next day, the finger was examined again, and the doctor reversed his decision to operate. The letter which he wrote his mother at that time describing the whole incident is redolent of his usual simple trust in the goodness of Our Lady to him, so that he would conclude: "Glory be to God and thanks to the Immaculata."

Later, while he was suffering in the hospital

at Krakow and was despaired of by the specialists, he revealed an utter dedication to Our Lady
that could only win from her an especial interest. He did not waver for a moment in his pledge
of trust. On one of those days when his fever
was dangerously high he was visited by his
brother, Father Alphonse. In his delirium he
began to call aloud, "Maria, Maria!" Alphonse
spoke softly to him in an attempt to comfort
him. But as the younger brother stood over
Father Maximilian, he heard the sufferer's weak
plea for his watch and eyeglasses. Strange request,
thought Alphonse to himself, but better to sat-
isfy this simple demand. When the glasses and
watch were brought to the sick man, he then
directed his brother to lay them before the statue
of the Blessed Virgin. Later on, explaining this
unusual request, he said: "The eyeglasses are the
symbol of my eyes; the watch, a symbol of time;
both of these are consecrated to her."

Father Maximilian's writings abound in refer-
ences to the complete trust that should be given
to the Immaculata, especially when all seems
lost. The phrase "abandon ourselves to the Immaculata" can be found repeatedly in his writings
and sermons. In his own life, the Immaculata
was never found wanting when he called upon
her. Characteristically, he wrote at one time:
"When it was clear that all other means were

powerless, when I was considered as lost and my superiors found me unfit for any work, it was then that the Immaculata appeared on the scene to gather up this poor debris which was not even fit for a waste basket. She took this good-for-nothing and she used it to spread the glory of God. For a moment, picture in your mind a great painter who painted his best work with a worn-out brush: Our Lady is that painter, and I am the brush." Father Maximilian always had the unswerving conviction that "there is no heroic act which we cannot accomplish with the help of the Immaculata."

Because of the chronic nature of his illness, Father Maximilian was transferred in January of 1920 to a sanatorium at Zakopane, Poland. He was to remain there until December, 1920— almost a year. But it was not to be an unfruitful year, by any means. It was a time of personal suffering, but through it all he gave himself to real priestly activity. After a short time there, he learned that some of the rest homes were entirely without religious attention, and that this was due in some part to certain directors who were inimical to religion. Father Maximilian began to visit these places, and it was not long before he was holding discussions and giving instructions. In a letter to his brother less than twelve days after his arrival there, he could already say, "We can thank the Immaculata because the worst enemy at Zakopane has gone to Confession." In the same letter he also wrote that he had baptized a Jew who had requested it and who died in spiritual bliss soon after. When the mother of the newly baptized learned of this, she complained indignantly to the authorities. Using this as a pretense, they tried to curtail Father Maximilian's activity, but with little success. The unassuming Franciscan found ways and means to continue his work of sanctifying souls.

While at this sanatorium he not only exercised his priesthood, but he also planned mentally and on paper for the future of The Militia of Mary Immaculate. However, in his letters to his brother he constantly reminded him that it was not necessary to plan too much; rather, a firmer trust in Our Lady would be more fruitful. In a letter dated November 1, 1920, he reminded Father Alphonse: "Let the Immaculata do what she wishes and whenever it pleases her, because I am her property and entirely at her disposal." A little over a month later he wrote: "As to the Militia, we are in the hands of the Immaculata, and we must do whatever she wishes, and this is made clear to us by obedience . . . Let us be careful not to do anything about The Militia of Mary Immaculate except what obedience permits, because otherwise, we shall not be acting as instruments of the Immaculata."

This devotion to obedience energized every day of Father Maximilian's life. Indeed, his superiors, especially in those early days, did not pamper him or agree with some of his proposals. In his regard they had used "much human prudence," with the result that his ideals for the spread of the Militia were restrained. This by no means embittered him; on the contrary, it strengthened his devotion to his vow of obedience. In another letter to his brother from Zakopane, he insisted upon obedience to their superiors in everything that they planned because "Perfection is based on the love of God, on union with Him, on conformity with Him. Our love of God is manifested by doing His Will, which is made known to us through the will of our superiors . . . I believe that the Militia must be founded on the road of contradiction: it is better that it be cultivated among distrust and adversities." Even with regard to his letters from Father Alphonse, he remarked on the beauty of obedience. It was customary for the parents of the students to send writing paper to their sons so that they might write more frequently than was usual. Mrs. Kolbe naturally was among the mothers who did this. Referring to this in a note from Zakopane, Father Maximilian wrote to his brother: "All that you write is good and Franciscan-like; but, if mother were not to send you additional writing-paper and stamps, it would be more Franciscan still."

Indeed, Zakopane produced the fruit of a more lively spiritual life for Father Maximilian. An insight into his inner life can be seen from the Rule of Life which he wrote for himself at Zakopane on September 20, 1920. It is included here in complete form because its clarity and simplicity of expression is characteristic of the clarity and simplicity of his whole spiritual life.

RULE OF LIFE TO BE READ EACH MONTH

1. "I must be a Saint and a great Saint.
2. "For the glory of God I must save myself and all souls, present and future, through the medium of the Immaculate.
3. "To flee 'a priori' not only mortal sin but also deliberate venial sin.
4. "Not to permit:
   a. That evil go without reparation and without being destroyed.
   b. That good fail to bear fruit and increase.
5. "Let your rule be obedience—the will of God through the Immaculate Mary—I am nothing but her instrument.
6. "Think of what you are doing; do not worry

about the rest, whether it be evil or good.

7. "Keep order, and order will keep you.

8. "Peaceful and kind action.

9. "Preparation—action—results.

10. "Remember that you are the exclusive, unconditioned, irrevocable property of the Immaculate Mary.

"As much as you are, as much as you have and can have: all—thoughts, words, actions and inclinations (good, indifferent)—are her absolute property.

"May she, and not you, do with everything as she wills.

"In like manner, all your intentions are hers. May she dispose of them, make and correct them, because she cannot make a mistake.

"You are an instrument in her hands; you must do, therefore, only what she wills.

"Obtain all things from her hands. Have recourse to her as the child to its mother. Trust in her.

"Be solicitous for her, for her glory, and for what pertains to her.

"You must admit that nothing is your own, but rather that all has been given by her. All the results of your labor depend upon your union with her. She is the instrument of Divine Mercy.

"My life (in every one of its moments), my death (where, when and how), my eternity: all is thine, O Virgin Immaculate. Do with me as you desire.

"All is possible to me in Him who is my comfort through the Immaculata.

"The interior life: first, it is entirely for my own sanctification, and then likewise for the sanctification of others."

Chapter 7

THE EDITOR OF THE
KNIGHT OF THE IMMACULATA

WHEN Father Maximilian felt better—although not cured by any means—he received permission from his superiors to return to Krakow. This was the beginning of a new era in his life. He decided to increase the membership of the Militia through the publication of a bulletin. The idea was proposed to his superiors, who gave him permission to publish the bulletin on this condition: he himself was to find the means to finance the project. The permission was all he needed. The rest he would do with the help of the Immaculata.

First, he decided to go begging. This was by no means easy for him. He himself tells how at one time he entered a stationery store to ask for an offering for his yet unpublished paper—but red-faced, he ended up purchasing an article instead of asking for the alms. Saintly man that he was, he reproved himself for not having repressed this instinctive flight from personal humiliation. So he tried again by entering a second store. But once again shame got the better of him. He left this place without even uttering a syllable. A third time he succeeded in making his request.

His begging on the whole was not successful, but money was not to be the sole problem. Father Maximilian nevertheless went ahead with the publication of his review. Difficulties faced him on all sides. He was no gifted writer, yet he had to write practically alone not only the first issue but also all the early issues. When it came time to pay the printers for the first issue of *The Knight of the Immaculata* (as he called his review), he had not a penny in his pocket. The poor priest did not know where to turn. Unfortunately, his Provincial Superior was in no better financial condition. His only contribution was a forthright rebuke: "That is where these absurd ideas will land you. Now you see what it is to attack the moon with a spade. And now it is up to you to extricate yourself without compromising your Friary."

But those who throw themselves blindly into the hands of God, as Father Maximilian did, can expect His help, though all others turn their backs. And Providence did step in! First of all, an unexpected generous offering came from Father Tobiasiewicz, a parish priest of St. Nicholas

Church in Krakow. But he still needed much more.

To whom could Father Maximilian turn? Quite instinctively, he wandered down to the altar of the Madonna of the Seven Dolors in the Basilica of St. Francis at Krakow. Throwing himself upon his knees, he told his "Immaculate One" the tale of his distress. He prayed long and confidently. As he was about to leave, his eye spotted an object on the altar cloth. "What could it be?" he thought to himself. He went up to the altar, and there it was—an envelope. He picked it up and read: "For thee, O Immaculate Mother." He opened it and found in it the exact sum of the debt which yet remained to be paid to the printers. Joyfully, he fell upon his knees and thanked Our Lady for the help. Even the Fathers of the Friary were quick to respect the unusual character of this incident. Without question, they allowed Father Maximilian to use this sum to pay his debt.

Financial problems faced him constantly. After the first issue appeared, he was not sure when the following would come out. In that first issue of *The Knight* he had published a note to readers: "Due to a lack of funds, we are not able to assure the readers of a regular edition of *The Knight*." But Father Maximilian worked and prayed and trusted.

As time went on, the number of subscribers increased. Since the other Fathers in the Friary did not take too ardently to this new project, he could expect little help from them. The result was that in those early days of his review, Maximilian had to sponsor the project practically alone. He not only wrote the articles and did the proofreading but now he had to give much time and energy to the fast-growing administrative affairs.

Chapter 8

EDITOR AND REVIEW
MOVE TO GRODNO

CONDITIONS at Krakow made it clear to
Father Maximilian's superiors that better
progress on the Review could be made at a different location. The various demands of publication, such as mailing lists, wrapping and
dispatch were too much for the quiet of the
Krakow monastery.

A new spot was easily found for the Review
and its editor. It was a small town at the other
end of Poland called Grodno. There, too, Father
Maximilian could expect little help from the
Fathers, who were for the most part elderly men
with parochial duties. However, a lay brother
was assigned to the priest-editor by Father Mel-
chior Fordon, the Superior of the Friary, who
was in complete sympathy with the editorial project.

Father Maximilian appreciated the assistance
and friendship of this Franciscan. In later years,
when he was informed that Father Fordon was

dying, he wrote to his brother, Father Alphonse: "Tell Father Fordon that when he is in Heaven, not to forget the direction of The Militia of Mary Immaculate, his brothers, their difficulties, and also myself."

But if some of Father Maximilian's hardships were eased by this kind superior, there were still many difficulties to be overcome at Grodno. The printing itself posed many problems. Strikes among the workers were frequent. Costs were high. Business conditions were so bad at Grodno that printing companies had to be changed no less than five times. The only solution to this problem, thought Father Maximilian to himself, was to get his own press. But how? What money he received as gifts had already been spent in printing the Review.

But as in other, similar instances, this was not to be an insurmountable obstacle for him. He looked around for a press and found one for sale at the Sisters of the Mother of Mercy at Lagiewniki. As with other projects, he received permission to purchase it, but on the condition that he find the means to finance the purchase. Again, Our Lady gave an evident sign of her protection. But the good Father had first to pay personally a contribution of humiliation.

At one of the evening recreations, a visitor from America, who later became Provincial of

the American St. Anthony Province, Father
Lawrence Cyman, was being entertained. Some-
one present hit upon the unhappy scheme of
injecting humor at Father Maximilian's expense.
The founder of *The Knight*, although anguished
by this open ridicule, simply lowered his eyes
and remained silent. But the American came to
his defense. He openly praised the publication
and suggested that a work of this nature should
receive not only the full support of all the Friars of that Friary, but even of the entire Province.
Then turning to Father Maximilian, he said: "To
help you, Father, I for my part give you this"—
and he handed him a check for $100.00, a very
sizable sum in those days.

The press was brought into the Friary, and
Father Maximilian set to work. Another Brother
had come to help him, thus increasing the editorial staff to three. These three took care of
everything—printing, management, packing,
mailing. Father Maximilian had to write and edit
the articles and then hurry off to help with the
printing—a slow process, 60,000 impressions for
5,000 copies of the Review. Besides this, he was
not freed from his parochial duties, nor were
the Brothers freed from the domestic care of the
Friary. The result was that they and their priest-
manager worked all day, even late into the night.

The 5,000 copies of the Review found ready

circulation—yet the financial returns were small. Readers began to ask for more copies. This meant new permissions from superiors to increase the output—and more work. The project soon became too big for the simple hand-press. So Father Maximilian began to look around for the means to buy a modern linotype. Naturally the older Friars decided against this, but still he got the necessary permission—provided he supply the money for it. And he did! How? We cannot say. The new linotype arrived. The staff was amazed at the many parts. Never before had they had any experience with this kind of machine. Then Our Lady entered again. In the face of the complexities of the linotype, a young mechanic, a specialist, turned up at Grodno and asked to be admitted to the community as a Brother.

The monastery at Grodno became a veritable workshop. Three places in the monastery were set aside for publication of *The Knight*: a room for administration, another for the press itself, and the third for dispatch facilities. As months went on, even this became inadequate and the printing staff had to ask for more room. More Brothers came and set to work with the printing group. It was beginning to be a community within a community. Father Maximilian was unofficially their director. They caught the fire of his

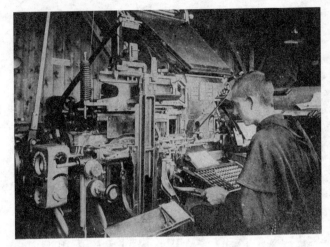

"The best inventions are meant to
serve HER most of all."

spirit; they worked and prayed. Production soared
year by year: 1924, 12,000 copies; 1925, 30,000
copies; 1926, 45,000 copies.

In 1926, Father Maximilian had a relapse.
Once more he was ordered by his superiors to
return to the sanatorium at Zakopane. Fortunately, by this time the press was paying for
itself.

While Father Maximilian was at Zakopane,
he learned that several of the Fathers at Grodno
had begun to look upon the press as a means
of income. This was far from the ideals of the
editor and founder. In a letter to his brother,
Father Alphonse, Father Maximilian described

pointedly the purpose of all his printing endeavors; the reason for the publication, he insisted, was to attract and conquer the entire world for Mary Immaculate. To this he added that the curse of St. Francis would certainly fall upon all their work if it were used as a means to assure to the religious an easy life.

Chapter 9

NIEPOKALANOW: THE CITY OF THE IMMACULATA

WHEN the editor returned from Zakopane, it became crystal clear to him that Grodno was no longer a suitable place for publication. First of all, considerable inconvenience resulted from housing under one roof religious dedicated to editorial work together with those obliged to the common regular observance of the Friary and to the duties of parochial care. Then, the isolated location of Grodno made inconvenient the business administration of keeping in contact with 60,000 readers, and it retarded the shipping of supplies.

For these reasons, Father Maximilian thought it wise to look around for a new location; he found just what he wanted only twenty-six miles from Warsaw. The land was owned by one Prince Drucki-Lubecki, whom the little Franciscan approached, but not before having placed a statue of Our Lady on the land. The property was offered by the Prince on fairly good terms, but they were not agreeable to Father Provincial. So Father Maximilian had to return to the Prince and tell him that the deal could not be made. Innocently, the Prince asked: "What am I to do with that statue?"

"Leave it where it is," answered the priest. The Prince thought for a moment and then said: "Take the land with it! I am giving it to you for nothing."

By October, 1927, Father Maximilian and some of the Brothers had arrived at the site of their future Friary. Primitive living quarters and a modest chapel were first put up. Life in those first days of October was by no means easy. The land was covered with snow. Often it was necessary for the Brothers to sleep without a roof over their heads. The small buildings that were going up hurriedly remained unheated. The people from the neighboring village pitied the Franciscans and brought them food and even kitchen utensils. Trunks served adequately as tables; the ground took the place of benches.

Father Maximilian worked and lived as the rest, despite his recent return from the sanatorium. The Brother's efforts showed results. By November 21, the place was ready to house all the machinery and the rest of the Brothers. The new location was of course dedicated to Our Lady—on December 7, 1927, the eve of the great feast of the Immaculate Conception. It was called Niepokalanow,* which is the Polish for "City of the Immaculata."

The new city grew up to sizable proportions. The first buildings, following the sleeping quarters and chapel, were those necessary for the printing of *The Knight*. In 1929, a college was built for the aspirants to the Order; then a building for novices; and one for the professed members. In due time, there was a hospital of a hundred beds, an electric plant and a fire department manned by the Brothers—all this by 1932. A radio station was erected in 1938, and an airport in the following year!

As the city grew, so did the religious community. Among the first friars at Niepokalanow, there were two priests, Fathers Maximilian and Alphonse, and 17 lay-brothers. By May, 1933, their number reached 364; in 1934, 500. In 1938 there were 762 Conventual Franciscans there; 13 of these were priests, 140 scholastics, and 609 lay-brothers—all specialists in their own field. Niepokalanow was the world's largest religious community.

Circulation increased with the number of buildings and religious. The 5,000 copies of *The Knight of the Immaculata* put out in 1922 at

---

*Pronunciation: *Nyep•oe•kah•lah´•nōōv*

Krakow and the 60,000 copies printed at Grodno in 1927 spiraled rapidly to 81,000 at Niepokalanow in 1928; 292,750 in 1930; to 800,000 in 1937; and to almost a million in 1939.

Nor was *The Knight of the Immaculata* the only review printed in the little city; there were nine others. In 1933 the Friars put out a monthly for youth called *The Little Knight of the Immaculata*. Its circulation reached 250,000. Next came the 40,000 copies of *The Chronicle of the Militia of the Immaculata*, which appeared each month since 1935 for the direction of the members of The Militia of Mary Immaculate. Also in 1935, a daily newspaper was published called *The Little Journal*. The weekday edition circulated 150,000 copies daily; whereas they sold 200,000 copies of the Sunday edition. In 1937 there appeared an edition of *The Knight of the Immaculata* for children, totaling 35,000 copies each month. Then there was a quarterly in Latin for priests, the *Miles Immaculatae*. When these Franciscans later established the City of the Immaculata in Japan, there appeared the *Missionary Bulletin of the Garden of the Immaculata*, a quarterly on the mission activity in Japan. For information on Niepokalanow directed to the Brothers themselves, there was a weekly paper called *The Echo of Niepokalanow*, and for the schools, an illustrated periodical, *Sporting Journal*.

Simultaneously with these publications, the Brothers took on other "odd jobs." They printed books, pamphlets, propaganda sheets—not only in Polish, but in many other languages, even Arabian. Small statues of Our Lady were made there and sent to all parts of the world, together with Lourdes water and other objects of devotion to Our Lady. The professors and students did theological research on Mariology. The Brothers were assigned to the various necessary activities: infirmarians, doctors, dentists, gardeners, tailors, carpenters, shoemakers, blacksmiths, mechanics, firemen—whatever would be needed to serve an independent community.

One can scarcely imagine the whirlwind of activity that constantly went on in this "City of the Immaculata." And all this was set in motion by an unassuming religious who was suffering from tuberculosis!

His letters, sermons and other writings are suffused with the idea of using all activity only to promote the glory of God and one's personal sanctification. No matter how mechanical the means, whether the press, movies, radio, airplanes, it was his intention to sanctify these things and use them for good. He was thoroughly convinced that all modern inventions were to be exploited for God's cause.

Even while he was a student at Rome, he had

this attitude. A friend, Father Pignalberi, recalled that while out walking one day, he and Father Maximilian argued to no end for the need of taking advantage of the potential good inherent in the movies. Father Maximilian was convinced that we must wake up and struggle for the camp against enemies of souls. In a similar vein he answered a canon visiting Niepokalanow, who, upon viewing the seething activity of the presses, had remarked: "If St. Francis were living today, what would he say to all this very costly machinery?"

"Why," answered Father Maximilian, "he would roll back the sleeves of his habit, he would start the machines top-speed and go to work as these good Brothers do, taking this modern way of spreading the glory of God and His Immaculate Mother."

But this activity should not be misunderstood. Father Maximilian, like his model, St. Francis of Assisi, was not an "activist" in any sense of the word. Certainly this twentieth-century Francis of Assisi did not lose his sense of values amid activity and progress. In his simple and inimitable way he summarized his concept of progress when one of the Brothers asked him: "Tell us, Father, in what does the true progress of Niepokalanow consist?

His answer reminds us of the response of St. Francis to Brother Leo regarding the notion of true joy. Father Maximilian replied, "If we were to have the latest machines, if we were to use all the technical improvements and all the discoveries of modern science, this would not yet be true progress. If our reviews doubled and even tripled their number, that would not be a proof of true progress."

"What is necessary then to have true progress? In what does the true progress of Niepokalanow consist?"

Forceful and eloquent was his reply. "Our exterior, visible activity, whether in the cloister or outside of it, does not constitute Niepokalanow, but the true Niepokalanow is in our souls. Everything else, even science, is only secondary. Progress is spiritual, or it does not exist. Consequently, even if we had to suspend our work, even if all the members of the Militia abandoned us, even if we had to disperse as the leaves swept by the autumn winds—if in our souls the ideal of Niepokalanow continued to grow, we could well say, my little children, that we were in full progress."

The *raison d'etre*, the very reason for the existence of Niepokalanow and all its activity, he always insisted, was first of all personal sanctification, and then the sanctification of others. On another occasion he put this very clearly: "The principal reason for Niepokalanow is the sanctification of the Brothers, our own sanctification. We must never forget this: we must first be Saints ourselves." Then he posed and answered another question: "But what is the specific character of Niepokalanow? Here it is: to convert and to sanctify souls under the protection and by the mediation of The Immaculata. Thus, it does not suffice to say simply: 'to convert and sanctify souls.' We must add: 'by the Immaculata.' These few words show the one specific difference. Everyone knows that the Virgin is the Mediatrix of all graces. What characterizes us is our absolute belonging to the Immaculata, the *raison d'etre* of Niepokalanow and of *The Knight of the Immaculata*."

What Father Maximilian preached as the ideal of Niepokalanow he certainly put into practice. Religious life there was severe. One time the Father Provincial pointed out to him that the life at Niepokalanow was more rigorous than elsewhere in the Order. To this he replied: "If Niepokalanow . . . were to favor laxity, or still worse, scandal, it would be better that God immediately send fire from Heaven to burn everything." The Brother candidates were scrupulously trained and screened. The result was a religious community of the highest spiritual caliber.

Despite their hectic activity, Fr. Maximilian and his co-workers spent, in accord with their rule, three and a half hours a day in community prayers and meditation. But this was not all. The Brothers were taught ever to realize that all their work was a prayer. To keep this truth constantly before their minds, they were to speak only when necessary during working hours and to use as a greeting, simply, "Mary." Their life was strictly a community life. There was no distinction between service enjoyed by priest and brother, between superior and subject. The only exceptions to the common life were the sick. They could have special meals and all the remedies they needed—no matter how costly. Indeed, here was the Franciscan life according to the ideals of St. Francis.

Chapter 10

JAPAN

BY 1930, just three years after its start, Niepokalanow was well established. Father Maximilian now began to look for new worlds to conquer. It was never his intention to limit his service to Poland. His was a universal ideal: "To conquer the entire world—all souls—for Christ through the Immaculata."

The choice of a new mission came to him very simply—as did all things. One day while riding in a train, he began a conversation with some Japanese students. As was his custom, he offered each a Miraculous Medal. In return the students gave him some small wooden elephants, which they carried as "good luck charms." This was enough for Father Maximilian. He could not forget these poor Godless souls.

One day, without warning, he approached his Minister Provincial and told him of his desire to go to Japan to start a City of the Immaculata there. Naturally, Father Provincial was startled, and his first impulse was to deter him. This was no time for Father Maximilian to leave. Niepokalanow needed him. He was its founder, the very soul behind the whole endeavor. These thoughts rushed through the Provincial's mind, yet he asked:

"Have you any money?"

He received the usual answer: "No."

"Do you know Japanese?"

Again, it was "No."

"Well then, do you have any friends over there, some help?"

"No, but I shall find them with the grace of God."

Permission was not given immediately, but ultimately the Provincial realized that Father Maximilian was merely requesting the logical development of what he had already begun.

On February 26, 1930, Father Maximilian, together with four especially zealous Brothers, was ready to leave for Japan. There were no sad farewells. Everything was done very quietly. As a matter of fact, at the moment of departure his own brother, Father Alphonse, was asleep in his room. Father Maximilian slipped into his room. He would not awaken his brother, who was not well; he simply kissed him lightly on the forehead and said quietly: "Sleep, my brother, sleep. Never was sleep more deserved in the service of the Immaculata! Good-bye . . . Who knows if we shall see each other again . . .!" They never met again on earth. Father Maximilian loved his brother, but for the love of the Immaculata and souls he could detach himself from his feelings. Even his mother did not receive a personal farewell. By this time, she was with the Sisters in Krakow. It was not until Father Maximilian was in Japan that he wrote: "You will forgive me, Mother, for not calling on you before going on my journey, but then I should have had to delay it, and you know that the missions are a matter of utmost importance."

When the little group left Niepokalanow, they first went down to visit Rome. In the Eternal City, they received the Apostolic Blessing from His Holiness Pius XI and the Seraphic Blessing from the Minister General of the Order of Friars Minor Conventual. The five missionaries were guests at the Seraphic College in Rome. When they arrived, Father Maximilian, in strict obedience to the rule of the Order, handed over his money to the Rector. The latter told him that he might retain it since he was not to remain long in Rome. But no—he placed it on a chair as he left the room. His devotion to holy poverty required this, and this he would do.

Father Maximilian always had a keen and conscious love for poverty. Even when he was building the living quarters at Niepokalanow, he commented on the simplicity of the plans: "Our houses should be so poor that, were our Father, holy Francis, to return, he would choose them as his dwellings." In this regard, he believed that the money necessary for the construction of more comfortable houses should be used for the sanctification of souls. His personal poverty was just as rigorous. His whole attitude toward material things reflected his utter trust in Providence and in the Immaculata. As it was, when the missionaries left Rome for Japan, they had only their tickets and fifty dollars.

On their way to Marseilles, whence they would embark during the first week of March, 1930, Father Maximilian and his companions made a stop-over at Lisieux, the burial place of St. Therese, and also at Lourdes. It was quite natural for him to be eager to make these visits: Lisieux enshrined the body of the Saint to whom he had entrusted all his conquests; Lourdes was a shrine dear to the heart of the one for whom he made these conquests.

When they sailed from Marseilles, the Franciscans really had no fixed destination in mind. They knew they wanted to work in the Orient, preferably Japan. That is all. The rest they left to the Blessed Virgin. They made stop-overs at Port Said, Saigon, Hong Kong and Shanghai. In this last-named place, Father Maximilian visualized many possibilities for a City of the Immaculata. It had good ports, railroads and general communications. Jurisdictional problems, however, would make this impossible.

The various religious communities had already been assigned certain sections for their respective mission activities. The section apportioned to the Franciscan Conventuals was badly located to serve as a City of the Immaculata. It was in the mountains and cut off from all communications. The Vicar Apostolic gave Father Maximilian permission to establish an administrative office in the city proper, but his hands were virtually tied against allowing him to set up the presses there and to build a friary. This problem proved unfortunate for the Franciscan missionaries, since during their short stay in Shanghai, a wealthy Chinese offered to place at their disposal his entire house. Other native Chinese offered to translate articles into Chinese for him and even to contribute toward expenses. But the jurisdictional regulations would have prohibited Father Maximilian from carrying out his main purpose—the establishment of a "City of the Immaculata." Therefore, by April 22 the Brothers were on their way to Japan.

The little group landed at Tokyo, where they visited the Apostolic Delegate. Father Maximilian laid his plans before this representative of

the Holy See. The idea of starting a City of the
Immaculata in Japan appealed very strongly to
the Apostolic Delegate. It was he who suggested
that the best location for their purpose would
be at Nagasaki, especially since the bishop there
was a Japanese, who would be able to assist in
language difficulties.

So the five missionaries were off to Nagasaki.
On arrival, they headed straight for the cathe-
dral. As they walked through the courtyard,
Father Maximilian noticed a statue of Our Lady.
This he considered a sign of success. *She* was
there to welcome him! Fortunately, the Bishop
had been acquainted with the community of
Franciscans since his student days in Rome. Moreover, he had been hospitably entertained as a
guest in their Friary at Assisi. It was like meet-
ing old friends. Father Maximilian explained his
plans to the Bishop in his straightforward and
simple way. The whole project appealed to the
Bishop, but in return he had one favor to ask
of this Franciscan who held doctorates in theology and philosophy. If Father Maximilian
promised to act as a professor in his seminary,
then he would give the group permission to
establish themselves in his diocese. It was quickly
agreed upon.

The Friars once again set to work. A piece of
land was rented in the suburbs of Nagasaki, and

"My little children, love the Immaculata . . ."

they built themselves a small wooden house. After a few days, a wealthy Catholic offered the financial help needed to purchase and install a completely equipped Japanese printing office. Thus was begun *Mugenzai No Sono*—"The Garden of the Immaculata."

Father Maximilian had just about unpacked when he expressed the hope of publishing an edition of *The Knight of the Immaculata* in Japanese for the month of May—just one month's time! This was impossible, thought the Bishop of Nagasaki to himself, but he told the priest to go ahead. The Franciscans had just acquired a press, but they could not speak Japanese, much less write it. But then Our Lady could be counted on to help her Knight as she had done on previous occasions. The students to whom he had been teaching philosophy offered to translate Father Maximilian's articles from Latin into Japanese. For this first issue, the five friars had to manipulate a makeshift hand-press until a motor press could be installed. All worked as if inspired, and they accomplished almost the impossible. On May 25, a telegram arrived at Niepokalanow, Poland; it read: "Today we are sending out the Japanese *Knight*. We have printing establishment. Hail the Immaculata!—Maximilian."

The hardships and trials of the early days of the Polish Niepokalanow now had to be relived in Japan. First of all, the Japanese clerics could not afford the time to continue their translation of Father Maximilian's articles. So, the Franciscan editor had to look around for new help. As an assistant editor, he found a Methodist who proved invaluable in translating into Japanese the Italian and English articles. Then a university professor, a pagan, offered to translate from German.

Soliciting subscriptions for the Review posed a knotty problem. Japanese custom and etiquette did not admit sending requests for subscriptions through the mail. Therefore, the Brothers had to distribute notices of the Review in the streets, workshops, trains and other public places. In return they received a card from the potential subscriber. Only after this quasi-personal acquaintance could they presume to ask for a subscription. Moreover, as they paced through these places day in and day out, they were at first suspected of Russian espionage and shunned. But once they had become familiar figures, a gracious reception was assured.

Amid all difficulties, the little community of five Franciscans grew. The first thing which had struck the eyes of Father Maximilian as they made their new abode was a statue of Buddha perched on the mountainside overlooking their property. This disturbed him no end. It had to be removed. And it was. To accomplish this, Father Maximilian bought the entire hill. This he paid for in installments, since he was, as usual, penniless at the time. The vacated lofty niche, so indicative of sway and power, he filled with a statue of Mary Immaculate.

Poor Buddha suffered somewhat at the hands of these Franciscans. We are told that one day the leader of the Buddhist priests visited the Friars out of courtesy, as well as interest in their work and life. Before leaving, he invited Father Maximilian to visit in return the Buddhist monastery. The good Friar accepted, seeing in such a visit an opportunity to acquaint these pagans with Our Lady. He certainly accomplished his goal. On bidding farewell to the Buddhist superior, he was assured that in the future, candidates to the Buddhist monastery would be asked whether they knew or wished "to know and love Mary the Mother of God!"

The simplicity and enthusiasm of the Friars attracted the Japanese. Vocations came from among their number. But, despite these and Brothers lately arrived from Poland, the new City of the Immaculata was slow in getting started. In 1934 there were twenty-four members of the Franciscan community at *Mugenzai No Sono*. This was a goodly number; seeds grow slowly in pagan lands. But it was not enough for its saintly founder, who envisioned, or hoped for, a growth comparable to that of the Polish Niepokalanow. During his stay in Japan and before his return to Poland in 1936, he accomplished the foundation of a Seraphic (Franciscan) Seminary, which at that time counted as many as twenty native aspirants to the Order.

The City of the Immaculata itself was built on a small hill north of Nagasaki, a twenty minute walk from the city. The first living quarters of the five Friars looked like the Convent at Rivo Torto, the very first home of St. Francis and his companions. The best that could be said for it was that it was a place to live. As late as December, 1931, almost two years after their arrival at Nagasaki, the Friars were still housed there. It was so bad that Father Maximilian described conditions thus: "We had a terrible snow storm last night. . . . I had to cover my head in order to sleep, for the snow fell in on me . . . in the dormitory of the Brothers, all was white . . ." And a letter of one of his brother helpers divulged that, "We began here as at Niepokalanow . . . sleeping on straw, eating on benches, and sitting on the ground."

Their poverty, especially in those first years, was extreme. Sacrifices were made without a murmur, for it seemed to matter little to these ardent Knights of Our Lady. They were happy with it all. They drank deeply of the spirit of Father Maximilian, who could write: "We are very happy because the Immaculata, our Mother, has given to us the grace of working for her, even of wearing ourselves out for her, and by these small sacrifices, of cooperating toward the salvation of these poor pagans. Indeed, there are some moments when our souls are vehemently homesick for the 'City of the Immaculata' in Poland, but only for a brief moment, for then we begin to think that we shall all meet in Heaven. With this, a flame of joy enters into our hearts, and a new and ardent desire for God consumes us." Here indeed are the thoughts of a soul in love with God and the Immaculata, a soul prepared to make any sacrifice, however difficult, to breathe his spirit into all—Christians and pagans.

Father Maximilian Kolbe with Japanese students.

Before leaving *Mugenzai No Sono*, it is inter-
esting to trace the subsequent cultivation of this
"Garden of the Immaculata." In August, 1945,
Nagasaki was leveled in the atomic bombing.
But the Blessed Virgin protected her beloved
City of the Immaculata from the slightest dam-
age whatsoever! During the war itself, the paper
shortage and government restrictions stopped the
publication of *The Knight*, but a year after the
war, in 1946, the Brothers were back on their
job. Fifteen thousand copies were printed and
distributed that year. Before World War II, the
Brothers reached production of 70,000 copies
per year.

Chapter 11

THE ORPHANAGE

AS a result of the atomic bombing in 1945, the environs of Nagasaki swarmed with orphaned children. They could be seen on any day walking aimlessly, seeking shelter and begging for food. The Brothers at *Mugenzai No Sono* were quick to extend arms of embracing love. They threw open their doors to these poor children. At least sixty of them were housed in The Garden of the Immaculata. But this was not enough, so an orphanage was built, which would give a home to a thousand children.

The soul of this new enterprise, this new field on which to conquer souls for the Immaculata, was Brother Zeno, one of the first five missionaries who had opened The Garden of the Immaculata in 1930. It is he who carried on the spirit of Father Maximilian in Japan. Even though he was an old man by this time, the orphans came to love him as a father. Afterwards, as he would walk the streets of Nagasaki, the Japanese, Christian and pagan alike, pointed him out as "The Father of the little orphans."

Chapter 12

INDIA

IN June, 1932, at the request of his Provincial in Poland, Father Maximilian set out for India to found another City of the Immaculata. At this time, he was plagued with an abscess on the back of his neck. But since the will of the Immaculata was made known to him by the wish of his superior, he obeyed with utter self-efface-ment. True, a "Niepokalanow" in India was fully in accord with his ideal to establish these "cities" wherever possible. In a letter written en route to India, he insisted: "I think that the Blessed Virgin gives to each one of us as many and as great graces as are necessary to carry out her plans. Consequently—but I must restrain myself—what I believe is that in every country a local 'Niepokalanow' is to be set up, using all the products of modern technique, for the best inventions are meant to serve *her* first of all."

On his way to India, Father Maximilian dis-embarked at Singapore. He was tempted to start a "City" there, but once again, jurisdictional restrictions interfered, so he continued his journey. By June 31, he was at Ernaculam, India. En route, he made the acquaintance of the Vicar General of the Malabar Rite in India. A fast friendship was struck, such that, when they landed in Ernaculam, the Vicar General insisted that Maximilian first discuss his plans with the Eastern Bishop. The little Franciscan so impressed him that the Bishop begged Father Maximilian to set up his "City" under his jurisdiction. A Syriac diocesan priest even offered to become a Franciscan to help begin this work. However, Maximilian could not accept this heart-warming generosity, since by law he had to turn to the Archbishop of his own Latin Rite.

While in the waiting room of the Latin Archbishop, he sat in view of a statue of his little friend of Roman days, St. Therese of Lisieux. As he spoke to her in prayer and reminded her of their agreement, a petal of a rose placed before her statue dropped off and fell at his feet. In his mind he thought, "Surely this is an evident sign that all will turn out well."

In fact it did. The Archbishop not only graciously received Father Maximilian, but personally drove him in his own automobile to a prospective site for the Indian City of the Immaculacata. Within five months, the same Archbishop made an official request to the Polish

Provincial to send priests and brothers to Ernaculam to establish there a City of the Immaculata. Thus ended Father Maximilian's personal apostolate in India. He had opened the way and prepared the groundwork. Unfortunately, prewar difficulties and the War itself delayed the opening of a City of the Immaculata in India.

When the indefatigable Maximilian returned to Japan, he did not remain there long. It was 1933, the provincial chapter year in Poland. His presence was requested there to explain all the developments in the East. At this Chapter, Father Maximilian was reappointed superior of the Japanese Mission.

Back once again in Japan, he set to work building a beautiful church in The Garden of the Immaculata. During this time Japanese publication reached the number of 65,000 copies annually. But as the days passed, Father Maximilian's health became worse. Hemorrhaging and spitting of blood were frequent. All symptoms pointed to an early death.

Chapter 13

RETURN TO NIEPOKALANOW

IN 1936, Father Maximilian was again called from *Mugenzai No Sono* to attend a provincial chapter in Poland. This time, he would return no more to Japan. Once at the chapter, having given his report on the Japanese Mission, he was elected superior of the Polish Niepokalanow. This appointment was the unanimous wish of all the Brothers at Niepokalanow. The Superiors who had succeeded him there were good men, excellent religious and fine administrators, but the Brothers felt that Father Maximilian was the soul of their apostolate.

But what a position to thrust upon a man of his physical incapacity! The weekly printing alone had mounted to one million copies. To administer this was not his only duty. There were others. There were workshops to be directed. Also, seven hundred religious, comprising priests, seminarians, novices, and lay-brothers—the largest religious community in the world—came under his guidance.

Fortunately, we possess many of the spiritual talks he gave to the religious during these years. He realized that time was short and that he had much to do. His most important assignment was the one he had set out to do when he established Niepokalanow—to make Saints of all its members. Categorically, he would say to the Brothers: "I demand that you be Saints, and very great Saints." On one occasion when he told this to the Brothers, he also explained very simply how it could be done. He asked for a piece of chalk. He smiled. He wrote: v = V. "Here is my formula," he said. "Do you understand it? The small v stands for *my* will (*voluntas* = "will" in Latin). The capital V is the Will of God. If you replace the equal sign by a plus sign, you have a cross: +. You do not want this cross, do you? Then, identify your will with that of God, who wants you to become Saints."

Indeed the formula was simple: v = V, but how difficult to realize in practice. Yet he was only asking the Brothers to learn something that he himself had learned and practiced for many years. That is why he could teach this theory of sanctity so well—he lived what he taught.

Another discussion with the brethren brings out the personality and inner life of the man. It is a revelation which helps us penetrate the little Father's inner spiritual life. He did not hesitate to reveal the attractions and consolations given to him by Our Lady in prayer so that he might bind to her more closely the men who were to continue the work at Niepokalanow after his death. This conversation took place on a Sunday evening, January 10, 1937. Supper had just been eaten. At the community hall, a religious play was to be dramatized by some of the Brothers. Just before they were to leave the refectory, Father Maximilian announced that all the friars were invited to the play, but that if any of the professed Brothers wished to remain in the refectory and chat with him, they could do so. The play was an unusual treat for the Brothers, so naturally most of them went to see it. Several remained behind. When they were settled at table, their Guardian began to speak. "My dear sons, now I am with you. Indeed, you love me and I love you. I shall die and you shall remain behind. Before leaving this world, I want to give you a remembrance . . ."

"You call me 'Father Guardian,' and that I am, because this is what I am in the Friary and in the print shops. But what am I above this? I am your Father, a father even more so than your earthly father who has given you your physical life. Through me you have received the spiritual life, and this is a divine life; through me you have received your religious vocation, which is more than physical life. Is what I say not true?"

Then one after another the Brothers agreed to this, saying: "If it were not for you, Father, *The Knight,* The City of the Immaculata, and all of us would not be here today." Another interposed: "By reading *The Knight,* I learned of the Franciscan apostolate." And so they went on.

Father Maximilian continued: "Indeed, I am called your Father. Do not look upon me, therefore, as a guardian or as a director, but simply as a Father. You have certainly observed that I have addressed you as my sons."

He then looked with intense kindness upon them, but something more seemed to be on his mind, something he was hesitating to say. Then lowering his head, he stammered: "My dear Sons, you know that I cannot be with you always. Therefore, as a remembrance, I want to tell you something. O my dear sons, if you only knew how happy I am. Yes, my heart is overflowing with happiness and peace. It is a happiness and a peace that can be found upon earth despite the difficulties of life. At the bottom of my heart an unspeakable calm reigns.

"My dear sons, love the Immaculata! Love her and she will make you happy. Trust in her without limit. Not all can understand the Immaculata. This can be gained only through prayer.

The Mother of God is Mary Most Holy. We know what 'Mother' means . . . She is the *Mother of God*. Only the Holy Ghost gives the grace of knowing His spouse, and this is to whomever He wishes and whenever He wishes.

"I had something else to tell you, but perhaps this is enough."

The Brothers begged him to go on.

"All right, I will tell you," he added quickly. "I have told you that I am very happy and filled with joy. And the reason for this: ". . . *I have been given an assurance of Heaven!* . . .

"O my dear Sons, love the Madonna. Love her as much as you know how and as much as you can."

As he made this confession, his eyes moistened with tears; there was a quiver in his voice. A moment of complete silence followed, a moment filled with wonder and amazement, but there was still a further revelation to come.

"Is it not enough for you to know all this?"

"Tell us more," whispered the Brothers. "Perhaps we shall never again have such a last supper."

"Because you insist," Father Maximilian continued, "I shall go on. *What I have said above happened in Japan.* That is all I shall say. Do not question me further on these things."

One or other of the Brothers pressed him for

the details of this revelation, but it was useless. Of this he would not speak again. He simply went on to tell them: "I have revealed my secret to you. I have done this so as to strengthen your courage and your spiritual energy for the difficulties ahead. There will be difficulties and trials, temptations and discouragement of spirit. When this happens, the memory of tonight will invigorate you and help you to persevere in the religious life. It will strengthen you for the sacrifices which the Immaculata will demand of you.

"My dear Sons, do not aspire to extraordinary things, but simply do the will of the Immaculata. May her will and not our will be done! I wanted very much to tell you these things, but even in doing this, I have desired only that her will be done. That is why I asked only those who were solemnly professed to stay here, and of their own free accord. Even while I was speaking to you, I held my rosary in my hand, counting off the *Aves* so that I might know whether or not to tell you what I did. I have told you what I thought might be told. I beg you to tell no one these things as long as I live. Please, promise this to me."

He was finished. There was silence. Deep in thought, the Brothers began to leave the room. In their hearts and on their lips were the words which did not have to be kept a secret: "Love the Immaculata! Love the Immaculata!" But their thoughts were filled with the prophetic words of their Father: "There will come difficult times, times of trial—of temptation, of discouragement." These were sombre warnings, yet they too were lightened by his further prediction that the memory of past graces would support them and urge them on to victory.

Surely as the Brothers left that room on the night of January 10, 1937, they did not visualize what really was to take place later. The War, which did come, came two and a half years later. At present there was peace in Poland; there was happiness and peace in the hearts of the Brothers of The City of the Immaculata. Time was to reveal to them the truth of their Father's words. Little by little, after 1939, were they to see the realization of these "difficulties, trials, temptations, discouragements"— and especially so the truth of the secret which had been revealed to Father Maximilian while he was in Japan. He had been given the assurance of Heaven, of final perseverance, but before that . . .

Chapter 14

THE FIRST ARREST

SEPTEMBER 1, 1939, the entire world was stunned by the news that the German Army had launched an attack on Poland. Within three weeks, the Nazis had taken the capital, Warsaw. Niepokalanow was only twenty-six miles from Warsaw. Father Maximilian saw clearly that this was the beginning of the end. Soon the Nazis would be marching into The City of the Immaculata. He had no doubt that it would be taken by the Germans. *The Knight of the Immaculata* was known to be anti-Nazi as well as anti-Communist. The conquerors would never overlook that.

Visualizing the troubles ahead, Father Maximilian decided that the Brothers should leave Niepokalanow. Some he told to try to reach their parental homes; others he directed to seek shelter in the various Franciscan friaries. Only sixty remained, five of whom were priests.

The planes began to drop their bombs. Scattered groups of German soldiers came and went.

They plundered whatever they wished: furniture, food, even crucifixes and statues of Our Lady. As yet Niepokalanow was not officially investigated. The remaining Brothers simply waited and watched their hard work of years destroyed. But in the midst of it all, Father Maximilian remembered the plight of holy Job, and he would repeat: "The Immaculata has given us all. She will take all away. She knows well how things are." These were the hours in which he could give to his Brothers the example of what he had preached.

By September 19, a strongly armed group of German police drove into Niepokalanow. The religious were ordered to assemble in the public square. Once assembled, they were loaded into trucks. They were not even permitted to return to their sleeping quarters to get extra clothes or other necessities. Twenty of the sixty who had remained at Niepokalanow were not present for the arrest, as they were in the infirmary suffering from wounds received during a bombardment. So they were spared this arrest. The destination of the prisoners was unknown, but the trucks headed toward the German border. It was not long before the prisoners found themselves in a German concentration camp, called Amtitz. This camp was not one to which the inmates were sent to be punished, one of those infamous penal colonies; it was a place of isolation for prisoners who were considered possible trouble-makers for the German regime. However, its prisoners had to face hunger and the suffering of sleeping outdoors, which was by no means easy in the cold Polish autumn. Those who were with Father Maximilian at Amtitz tell how he buoyed up their courage by his resignation to this plight, how he smiled paternally upon them despite everything.

This picture of Father Maximilian Kolbe was taken at the time of his internment by the Gestapo, Warsaw, 1939.

After this group of Brothers was arrested, the German Army marched eastward. Niepokalanow was quickly turned into a hospital by the Germans. Gradually, some of the Brothers who had left before the arrest returned to Niepokalanow, where they assisted the wounded. The Germans were the overseers of the temporary hospital, but they would not turn a hand to save the warehouses from pillage; food, clothing, paper, construction material gradually disappeared. Niepokalanow was quickly stripped of everything. But the Brothers carried on.

The Polish campaign came to a quick end. Western Poland, in which Niepokalanow lay, was occupied by the German conquerors. Life began to resume some sort of normal proportions. Prisoners were being released, and among these were Father Maximilian and the Brothers. By December 8, the Feast of the Immaculate Conception, he was back at Niepokalanow. His heart bled at the sight of such destruction. Even the statue of Our Lady which had stood at the entrance of Niepokalanow was gone. But once again the Knight of Our Lady rolled up his sleeves and set to work. Would there always be these beginnings?

The chapel was made presentable so that Perpetual Adoration of the Blessed Sacrament could be resumed. A statue of Our Lady was found in the debris, and he had this set up at the entrance the City. All this was done on the very day of their return. In the following days they worked and worked, but this time it was for the necessities of life. Day by day there could be seen some new place restored: a carpenter shop, a dairy, a workshop . . .

Each day also welcomed the return of more Brothers. Soon there were three hundred of them. Others could not return because they were sought by the Gestapo as special suspects because of the important positions they had held in the publishing of the reviews and papers.

Before the month of December ran out, Niepokalanow was turned into a concentration camp; approximately 2,000 prisoners were sent there. This increased the hardship and the poverty. But it presented an excellent opportunity for these Franciscans to spread the knowledge and love of God. The Brothers took care of the sick; the Fathers acted as chaplains. The priestly ministry to which Father Maximilian dedicated himself in those days reminded him of the work he had done at Zakopane. He loved this work. He always had a tender feeling for the sick, easily understandable in view of his own chronic sickness.

But a deeper reason than his own suffering made him love the sick: he was firmly convinced that "The sick work very much for the cause of the Immaculata." He understood well that it is easy to lose one's sense of values in the pride of accomplishments which are the fruit of good health; but sickness diminishes the danger of this pride, and one learns to understand dependence upon God for all things. He used to say that if the sick can do so much for the Immaculata by their patience, humility and perseverance, how much the more "do they work whom death has taken? After we get to Heaven, we shall understand this better, because there one works with both hands; while here on earth we must care for ourselves with one hand, in order not to fall, and thus we can work with only one hand."

Even under the eyes of their German guards, the Franciscans began to reorganize their community. A grapevine system was set up among the Brothers. In this way Father Maximilian was kept informed of the whereabouts and conditions of the Friars separated from Niepokalanow. This system was also useful in keeping intact their religious ideals.

Father Maximilian wrote numerous letters which were permeated with his ardent spirit. In these the absent Brothers were urged to continue their missionary activity of conquering hearts for the Immaculata, even in these adverse conditions, and they were reminded that they could fruitfully offer their sufferings for this purpose. Ever the Guardian of his Friars, Father Maximilian warned them of the pitfalls which were open to them as a result of their living outside the friary. However, he went on to console them with the promise that a special grace to overcome tepidity would certainly be given them if they did not depend upon their own will, if they remained men of prayer and faithfully observed their vows.

As the months passed, more Brothers returned. Soon there were 600 of the original community living at Niepokalanow. By the beginning of 1940, Father Maximilian was receiving new members into the novitiate. The seminary courses were again taught. Then it was suggested to him that he might even receive permission to put out *The Knight*. The idea appealed to him. He applied for this permission, and it was granted.

Thus on the Feast of the Immaculate Conception, 1940, the first and only issue came out during the war. In this Father Maximilian wrote his last article. It was his last will and testament to his Knights throughout Poland. Brief, with the calm pointedness of one who knows he has not long to work for God, it breathed forth his soul and the ardent love he had for the Immaculate One. In his clear and simple style he wrote:

"Once again, December 8th is approaching, the Feast of The Immaculate Conception.

"Whoever can, should receive the Sacrament of Penance. Whoever cannot, because of prohibiting circumstances, should cleanse his soul by acts of perfect contrition: i.e., the sorrow of a loving child who does not consider so much the pain or the reward as he does the pardon from his father and mother to whom he has brought displeasure.

"Therefore, this desire is good: to purify our souls on the feast of her whose soul was never stained.

"Those souls who have the privilege of knowing her intimately, love her fervently. Most carefully they seek continually to purify and refine their conscience and in this way to resemble her more and more, to attach themselves to her, to please her.

"But in what does the evil which stains the soul consist?

"If virtue consists in the love of God and of all that which springs from love, evil will be all that which is opposed to love. This the soul should always fear; it should therefore desire to be ever more immaculate, after the example of its beloved Lady and spiritual Mother.

"Those souls consecrated to her in a special way ought to renew their offering on that day.

Also, the members of The Militia of Mary Immaculate should renew their act of consecration— by which they may gain a plenary indulgence, that is, the remission of all the punishment which, after the sin has been forgiven, they must expiate here on earth or in Purgatory.

"On the Feast of the Immaculate Conception, having received the Sacrament of Penance and having made the act of consecration, and also having thereby gained the remission of punishments, the soul should more easily find interior peace, even joy, for the soul knows that no cross, whether from within or from without, can come without God's permission, which is that of a truly loving Father. He allows only what is for the greater good of souls as far as eternal salvation is concerned.

"May the fruit of this feast be an ever greater purity of conscience and an ever deeper peace. May it be a peace of resignation to Divine Providence. May it be an ever more generous readiness in the most perfect fulfillment of duty, thereby giving tangible proof of love for our spiritual Mother and our heavenly Father.

[Signed] Maximilian Kolbe"

Chapter 15

SECOND ARREST

THIS freedom was not to be enjoyed for long. Father Maximilian had returned to Niepokalanow on December 8, 1939: there would be fourteen months of freedom, and then his final arrest. February 17, 1941 was the day on which the Gestapo arrived for a second time and gave the order that all the religious assemble in the square. By this time there were over six hundred of them, six of whom were priests. Maximilian and four of the other priests were immediately placed under arrest. These five were supposedly dangerous to the safety of the German troops. Moreover, Father Maximilian was accused of helping the Polish Resistance Movement by giving the service of his press to print clandestine newspapers. This was not true. Factually, when he had been approached by the Poles for this purpose, he refused most emphatically. He knew that to help this cause would be to jeopardize the work of the apostolate. He did know that this underground resistance was going on, but when questioned, he refused to give information on the subject to the Germans.

Thereupon the five prisoners were taken to Warsaw and confined in the historic prison of Pawiak. Father Maximilian remained there until May, 1941, just three months. When his confreres were sent to Auschwitz in early April, he was ill with pneumonia and therefore was left behind. His Provincial tried to secure his release, as did also twenty of the Brothers, who offered themselves as hostages in his place. But this was all in vain.

In early March he had been transferred to a cell in which there were two other inmates. One of these gave an eyewitness account of the following instance of the Franciscan's heroic fortitude.

Father Maximilian was still wearing his black Franciscan habit. A few days after he was assigned to this cell, an inspection was made by the head section guard. When the guard saw Father Maximilian in his religious habit, he stopped short. His face reddened with anger. He looked at him momentarily, then turned his questioning to the cellmate. This done, he approached the Franciscan and snatched at the crucifix which was hanging from the white cord around his waist. "And you believe in this?" he shouted in the face of Father Maximilian. And the calm reply:

"Most certainly, I believe in it!" At this the guard turned red with rage and brutally struck the priest in the face. Three times he repeated his question, emphasizing it with fresh blows. Three times came the same reply. His cellmate was almost driven to throw himself at the cruel bully, but he restrained himself, realizing the futility of such action. Despite the blows, the Franciscan remained perfectly calm, and were it not for the welts rising on his face, one would scarcely have known that the incident had occurred.

After the guard left, the poor victim began to walk slowly up and down the cell. He knew that his cellmates were irritated and excited. To calm them, he said: "There is no reason for excitement. You have enough serious troubles of your own, so it is foolish. All this is for our 'Mammina.'" Shortly after, a Polish guard who had witnessed this occurrence brought prison clothes to Father Maximilian, for he knew that the priest's habit and crucifix aroused the wrath of the head guard.

Shortly after this, Father Maximilian again succumbed to pneumonia. He was of necessity taken from the cell and lodged in the infirmary. The next time he was heard from, it was May 1. We have two notes which he wrote to the Brothers at Niepokalanow on that day. In the first, he simply advised them that he could receive food packages on the first and twentieth of each month. The second note was an acknowledgment of a package sent at Easter time. From this letter it is learned that Father Maximilian had been released from the prison infirmary and put to work in the library.

On May 12 the prison head ordered Father Maximilian to write to the brothers for a civilian suit. Still faithful to his vow of poverty, he told the Brothers that it would not be necessary to send new trousers along, as "mine are still in good condition." However, he did need a working jacket, a vest and a woolen scarf. He probably knew that he was destined for another concentration camp.

Indeed, a few days after this the Immaculata was to lead the priest into the camp where he was to become a martyr of charity. This spot, paradoxically, was to become sacred to him, for here his Lady was to hand him the red crown which she had held out in that vision of his youth.

Chapter 16

AUSCHWITZ

THE concentration camp of Auschwitz— Oswiecim in Polish—is situated in Poland where the Sola River meets the Vistula, close to the old German city of Auschwitz. The camp itself, considered one of the most horrible of German concentration camps, could hold 200,000 prisoners at the most. Its name among Poles— the camp of death, or the sepulchre of the Poles— was well earned, for it is estimated that of the millions of victims who died there, most were Polish. Father Maximilian was among the 400 who arrived from Pawiak on May 28, and with him were fourteen other clergymen. What happened to Father Maximilian during the next two and a half months has been reported by six eye-witnesses, three of them fellow priests. The fourth was another prisoner, who, as we shall see, befriended Father Maximilian in the prison. The fifth was a young sergeant whose place he took in the starvation cell, and the sixth was a Polish orderly in the death block where the priest died.

After they left Pawiak prison, the four hundred unfortunates were crowded into cattle cars at the Warsaw station in the early morning. They arrived in the evening at the Auschwitz railroad depot, about a mile from the camp itself. Goaded on by the gun butts of the SS and the trained hounds who snapped at their heels, the prisoners had to travel the mile almost constantly on the run. Hungry and weak—especially so Father Maximilian, who was not yet fully over the effects of pneumonia—they were lined up for roll-call in the square at the camp. As a prisoner's name was called, he had to leave the group and run to the line-up of those already accounted for. On the run, he was beaten with cords weighted with lead and was frequently tripped by the guards. After this, the four hundred were herded for the night into a hall with a floor space of 27 by 95 feet. It was a night made dreadful by foul odors and the lack of fresh air. The following morning, all of them were stripped of their clothing and in a group showered with icy water. In place of their own clothing they were then given old and ragged clothes, many of which were still blood-stained from their former wearers. Once again they were assembled for roll-call and for assignments to prison blocks, according to the type of work they would have to do. Jews and priests were singled out for special treatment. The former were candidates for slow but certain death; the latter were given hard labor. Father Maximilian and his fellow priests were to go to Block 17.

All day long they waited in their new quarters for the next move. But nothing happened. The following day, the Commandant of the camp, Fritsch by name, appeared at Block 17. The gruff command snapped out: "Come along with me, you lazy priests." Along they went, and after a tiring wait Fritsch handed them over to "Bloody Krott," a section head notorious for his blood-thirsty cruelty. Their new guard was instructed: "Take these useless parasites of society and teach them what it means to work."

"Leave everything to me," Krott replied. And he lived up to his sneering promise!

Poor Father Maximilian, weak and sick, a consumptive for many years, was first assigned to dig sand and stones for the construction of a wall around a crematory. He could have done this work—for indeed, the many years in the print shop had taught him how to work—but the barrows had to be brought from one place to the other on the run, or else he would be struck by the guards stationed at thirty foot intervals.

This work lasted only a few days. He was next assigned to a crew reclaiming swamp land about two and a half miles from the camp. Here he cut tree trunks and then carried loads two or three times a normal weight over rough and rutted ground. If he slackened on the way, he was flogged without mercy. On one occasion, he was beaten so badly that his fellow priests were ready to help him, but he simply replied: "Do not expose yourself to the same treatment. The Immaculata is helping me. I will manage."

Suffering was indeed nothing new to Father Maximilian. The years of trial sustained under his weakening tuberculosis and the difficult days spent building his Niepokalanow in Poland and Japan had hardened him to its sting. And then, had he not learned to make the best of suffering, to use it as a means for personal sanctification? Even while at Auschwitz, he could still console his fellow prisoners by telling them how God tries souls by suffering and thus prepares them for a better life. "They may kill our bodies," he would say, "but they cannot kill our souls . . . if we die, we shall die peacefully, resigned to the Divine Will."

A will such as this, strengthened by grace, could not be broken, no matter how much his guards might try. And try they did. Krott especially hated this priest who loved all men. The placid and resigned acceptance of every torture by this worn-out Franciscan drove the vicious

Krott almost to frenzy. One day, he resolved to break this indomitable will once and for all.

Father Maximilian was burdened with an extra heavy load of wood and then ordered to run. When he tripped and fell to the ground, he was kicked in the face and stomach and struck with a club. Almost unconscious, he could hear ringing in his ears: "You do not want to work, you lazy creature! I'll teach you what it means to work!" Not satisfied with this cruelty, Krott ordered the priest extended on the trunk of a tree and given fifty blows by the stronger guards. The victim did not move, so he was thrown into the mud and covered with brushwood. When he revived, Krott ordered him to march the two and a half miles back to camp. But he could not make it. He had to be put on a cart and pushed home. The following morning, it was impossible for him to get out of his bunk for work. He was brought to the hospital and there his condition was diagnosed as "pneumonia with general exhaustion."

At the hospital Father Szweda, one of the priests who had come with him from Pawiak, happened to be an infirmarian. When he heard that Father Maximilian was there, he went to visit him. He found him, but Father Maximilian was a horrible sight to see. His face was disfigured, his eyes swollen, his body burning so violently with fever that he could not open his mouth to speak.

After a few days, Father Szweda found Father Maximilian a bit rested but still in a raging fever. The infirmarian priest later reported that the Franciscan patient astonished the doctors and infirmarians by his manner of accepting suffering. He did not fail for a moment to resign himself completely to the will of God; often he was heard to repeat: "For Jesus Christ I am ready to suffer more. The Immaculata is with me and is helping me."

Father Maximilian was in the hospital about three weeks, and here again he found ample opportunity to exercise his priestly powers. He had been assigned a bed near the entrance of the ward, and as a body was carried out, one could see the hand of Father Maximilian gently rise in conditional absolution. As he grew well, he began to hear Confessions, but this had to be done in secret, frequently during the quiet of the night. Near the end of his stay he could get around to visit others; often the good "Little Father" could be heard talking about the goodness of his Lady Love, the Immaculata.

Frequently, after his work was done, Father Szweda would steal over to visit his friend. When they met, Father Maximilian would embrace him like a child and talk to him about the Immaculata. "She is the true consoler of all. She hears everyone. She helps everyone."

One day Father Szweda brought Father Maximilian a cup of tea which he had saved especially for him. But Father Maximilian refused it: "Why should I be an exception; the others don't have any!" Indeed, he loved these "others," and they loved him, whom they called endearingly their "little Father."

By July 3 Father Maximilian was ready to be sent back to camp, but since he was still running a fever, he was assigned to Block 12, which was restricted to invalids. Here he was not assigned any heavy work, but he was made to pay for this leniency. The food ration was reduced to half the normal amount. This, of course, increased the death rate, a state of affairs Father Maximilian seized upon immediately by assisting the dying whenever he could.

While in Block 12, Father Maximilian met a former assistant editor of one of the papers at Niepokalanow, now serving as the foreman of a potato-peeling detail. This man pulled some strings to have Father Maximilian assigned to his crew. While the two worked together, Father would encourage his superior by telling him to trust in the Immaculata. One day he went on to predict, "You young men will live, but I will not survive this camp."

And how true was his prediction. Despite the "wire-pulling" of his friend, Father Maximilian was transferred from Block 12 to Block 14. This was about July 24 or 25. Here, in a few days, he was to make the greatest sacrifice one man can make for another.

It was July 30 or 31 when whisperers along Block 14 rasped that one of its inmates had escaped. A sickening feeling clutched the prisoners of that Block as they heard this news. These men knew the penalty for an escape—twenty men of the hapless Block would be sentenced to slow starvation and inevitable death.

That night the men of Block 14 slept very little; they were tortured by the thought: "Will it be I?" The long hours of the dark night slowly ushered in the light of dawn. The prisoners of the entire camp assembled for roll-call. Commandant Fritsch solemnly announced that the prisoner had not been found. He then ordered that all groups go to their respective assignments—all except the men of Block 14.

All day long the men of this Block had to stand at attention in the broiling hot sun. They were not permitted even a cup of water. Then, one by one, they began to faint, but not the frail little priest who had been expected on several occasions to die from tuberculosis and pneumonia. He kept standing and waiting.

The hours passed slowly. It was torture, this waiting and wondering. About three o'clock in the afternoon they were allowed to rest for a half an hour, and soup was given to them. This was the only food they had had all day, and for some of them it would be their last meal. This respite quickly over, they stood once again at attention until evening, when the other prisoners returned from their various assignments.

Once again there was a general assembly. All the prisoners of the camp stood at attention. Then, in the solemn silence, the prison Commandant appeared for inspection. Slowly and deliberately he approached the group from Block 14. Terror and fear darted from their eyes. This was the fatal moment. Within the next few minutes they would learn whether they were to live or to die. Fritsch began to speak: "The fugitive has not been found. In his place, ten of you will die in the starvation cell. The next time, twenty will be condemned."

Then he began to select the ten. It was a heartless business, yet to him it was as simple as picking apples out of a basket. He viewed the first row, one after the other. He selected almost at random and ordered the condemned to step forward. The Commandant's assistant wrote down the number of each victim.

Fritsch continued the process until ten men

had stepped forward. Father Maximilian was not among the group. Suddenly, one of the victims began to sob in broken words: "My poor wife and my children, I shall never see them again!" The condemned were then ordered to remove their shoes. The young man still wept for his wife and children. A horrible fate! To be condemned to slow death by starvation and thirst.

Another command was given: "Left face!" When the men turned, they could see the place of their death, Block 13. They were ready to march when suddenly a figure stepped forward from the ranks of Block 14. Stooped and worn, he walked directly to the Commandant, stopping just in front of him. Fritsch had never seen anything so boldly done since he was there. He quickly put his hand on his gun, prepared to meet an attack—by a frail, exhausted prisoner. Almost frightened, Fritsch commanded: "Stop!" and then snarled: "What does this Polish pig want?"

The prisoner halted; it was "Little Father Maximilian." Calmly, with a rapturous smile lighting up his eyes, he looked into the face of Fritsch. Then very softly, so softly that only those standing close by could hear, he said: "I want to die in place of that father of a family. I beg you to accept the offer of my life."

Fritsch was dumbfounded. All he could stammer was: "And why?" The reply was prompt and simply put.

"Because I am old and useless. My life is not worth anything, while he has a wife and family." As one author has noted, Father Maximilian thus offered Fritsch a Nazi-type reason to change his mind and yet save face.

Fritsch was up against something new. It was obvious that he had lost command of the situation. He asked:

"Who are you?"

His eyes cast down, the Franciscan solemnly answered: "A Catholic priest."

There was a moment of silence. Father Maximilian waited. Fritsch did not speak, but simply motioned with his hand, signifying that he accepted the offer. Father Maximilian stepped up to the ranks of the condemned. The assistant coldly jotted down his number—16670, and then he erased the number of the father of the family, who was told to step back. Another order was given: "March!" and the condemned men, a priest now among their number, proceeded to the place where they would die.

"I offer my life for this man . . ."

Chapter 17

THE DEATH HOUSE

BLOCK 13, the death chamber of Auschwitz, situated on the right side of the camp, was surrounded by an eighteen-foot wall. The cells were underground. It was to one of these cells that Father Maximilian came on July 31, 1941. When he and his nine companions arrived, they passed by a cell which housed twenty other victims of a previous starvation sentence. These latest ten were locked in a cell of their own. As the SS guard clanged the door behind them, he laughed and mercilessly reminded them: "You will dry up like tulips!" What he said, he meant; from that time on, these prisoners received neither food nor drink.

This was a strange group. They were so different from the others who had died in the same way. Instead of tears and pleas coming from their cell, there was heard the sweet prayer of the Rosary and hymns to the Blessed Virgin. The death cell seemed more like a chapel. Sometimes the victims were so engrossed in their prayers

that when the SS guard opened the cell for
check-up, they did not know he was there until
he gruffly shouted for silence. What an influ-
ence this priest wielded over his companions in
death! As the days passed, the victims died one
by one—some from hunger and thirst, others
from a kick in the stomach in answer to their
pitiable plea for water.

The Polish interpreter and orderly who visited the cell every day reported that Father Maximilian never asked for anything and that it was
he who encouraged the others not to despair.
As the days went on, their prayerful voices became
weaker and fainter. Almost to the end, Father
Maximilian could be seen on his knees in prayer.
He was truly remarkable. The SS guards knew
of the sacrifice he made; they saw him calmly
accept this torture. Even they learned to respect
him, so that often they were heard to remark:
"This priest is really a gentleman. We have never
before seen a prisoner like him."

Only four prisoners survived the second week.
Among them was the frail, consumptive Father
Maximilian. However, this group had lasted too
long. The cell was needed for other victims. So
the prison infirmarian was called in to end their
lives with an injection of carbolic acid. He
approached Father Maximilian, who was seated
on the floor with his back resting against the

wall, his head fallen a bit to the left side. The priest saw him come, and with the words "Ave Maria" on his lips, he submitted his left arm to the executioner. In a moment it was all over. The date was August 14th, the vigil of the feast of Our Lady's Assumption.

The Polish orderly witnessed the whole proceeding, up to the time of the carbolic acid injection. Then, unable to stand any more, he fled. When he returned, Father Maximilian was dead. The orderly reported: "When I opened the iron door, he was no longer alive, but he seemed as if he were still alive. His face was unusually radiant. His eyes were opened wide, staring into space. He seemed as though in rapture. I shall never forget that sight."

With the help of another, the orderly carried Father Maximilian's body to the morgue, where it was washed and placed in a coffin. It was then burned in the crematory—a routine procedure, but it almost seemed as though these men would be satisfied with nothing less than a complete holocaust of Our Lady's Knight.

Father Maximilian was dead. But he had died as peacefully as he had lived. In death his face was radiant, his eyes wide open and expectant, fixed as it were upon the promised vision of God and of His Immaculata. The young boy's dream of the red crown of martyrdom had come

Fr. Maximilian Kolbe receives the fatal injection—August 14, 1941, vigil of the feast of the Assumption of Our Lady. (Painting by M. Koscielniak.)

true in a surprising manner. With soulful humility he had prayed for it, with calm patience he had awaited it. And when it was offered at long last, he reached out for it with saintly courage and embraced it in the clasp of eternal union.

EPILOGUE

FATHER Maximilian's holiness of life was admired and acclaimed even while he was alive. After his heroic death, his sanctity was praised spontaneously not only by his confreres, but by prelates and faithful alike. Especially after the end of World War II in 1945, reports of graces and favors received through his intercession came in from widely distant places. An amazing number of books, pamphlets and articles appeared in many languages detailing the incredible life and deeds of this modern son of St. Francis.

During the ensuing years, the necessary ecclesiastical investigations were carried out by the Church. These culminated in the beatification of Father Maximilian Kolbe as a confessor in 1971, and in his canonization on October 10, 1982 as a martyr.

The work of St. Maximilian Kolbe is carried on in the United States by the Franciscans at Franciscan Marytown in Libertyville, Illinois. This is the American headquarters of the Knights of the Immaculata.

Photo of Fr. Maximilian Kolbe in 1940, the year before he was sent to Auschwitz.

St. Maximilian Kolbe—canonized on October 10, 1982.

If you have enjoyed this book, consider making your next selection from among the following . . .

At your Bookdealer or direct from the Publisher.
Call Toll Free 1-800-437-5876.

Prices subject to change.